RACHEL CARSON
A Voice for the Natural World

"One way to open your eyes to unnoticed beauty is to ask yourself, 'What if I had never seen this before? What if I knew I would never see it again?'" — Rachel Carson

Life Portraits

RACHEL CARSON
A Voice for the Natural World

By Charles Piddock

Gareth Stevens
Publishing

Please visit our web site at **www.garethstevens.com.**
For a free catalog describing Gareth Stevens Publishing's list of high-quality books,
call 1-800-542-2595 (USA) or 1-800-387-3178 (Canada).
Gareth Stevens Publishing's fax: 1-877-542-2596

Library of Congress Cataloging-in-Publication Data
Piddock, Charles.
    Rachel Carson: a voice for the natural world / by Charles Piddock.
        p. cm. — (Life portraits)
    Includes bibliographical references and index.
    ISBN-10: 1-4339-0058-0   ISBN-13: 978-1-4339-0058-7 (lib. bdg.)
    1. Carson, Rachel, 1907-1964—Juvenile literature. 2. Biologists—United
States—Biography—Juvenile literature. 3. Environmentalists—United States—
Biography—Juvenile literature. I. Title. II. Series.
    QH31.C33P53   2009
    333.95'16092—dc22
    [B]   2008031544

This edition first published in 2009 by
Gareth Stevens Publishing
A Weekly Reader® Company
1 Reader's Digest Rd.
Pleasantville, NY 10570-7000 USA

Executive Managing Editor: Lisa M. Herrington
Creative Director: Lisa Donovan
Cover Designer: Keith Plechaty
Interior Designers: Yin Ling Wong and Keith Plechaty
Publisher: Keith Garton

Produced by Spooky Cheetah Press
www.spookycheetah.com
Editor: Stephanie Fitzgerald
Designer: Kimberly Shake
Cartographer: XNR Productions, Inc.
Proofreader: Jessica Cohn
Indexer: Madge Walls, All Sky Indexing

The publisher wishes to thank Frances Collin Literary Agent for permission to publish
excerpts from Rachel Carson's works.

Printed in the United States of America

1 2 3 4 5 6 7 8 9 12 11 10 09 08

TABLE OF CONTENTS

Rachel Carson felt that the very survival of nature was at stake when she testified against the unregulated use of pesticides at a Senate hearing on June 3, 1963.

CHAPTER ONE

The Writer Speaks

O N June 3, 1963, hearing room 102 in the Senate Office Building in Washington, D.C., was overflowing with reporters, camera crews, officials, and spectators. It was so crowded that there was barely space to move. Yet the room was strangely quiet. All attention was focused on the two people facing each other at separate tables.

Senator Abraham Ribicoff, chairman of the Senate Subcommittee on Environmental Hazards, sat at one table. At the other was Rachel Carson, author of *Silent Spring*. She was there to convince Congress to pass laws eliminating a danger that she believed threatened the entire country. She was there to present a case for banning the use of certain chemical pesticides.

Rachel had already presented her case dramatically and in frightening detail in *Silent Spring*. She had shown, in case after case, how chemical pesticides, especially Dichloro-Diphenyl-

Trichloroethane (DDT), were poisoning America. Rachel showed how insects absorbed the poisons, and how the animals that ate the insects became contaminated. She demonstrated how the chemicals washed into streams and made their way up the entire food chain. If limits were not put on the use of pesticides, Rachel argued, there would soon be a truly "silent spring." She wrote:

> *There was once a town in the heart of America where all life seemed to live in harmony with its surroundings ... Then a strange blight crept over the area and everything began to change ... There was a strange stillness ... The*

Farmers made great use of DDT in the late 1940s. They often sprayed the chemical from low-flying planes to protect farm animals from pests.

A "Miracle" Pesticide

Soon after the end of World War II (1939–1945), chemical companies began promoting the everyday use of pesticides. They had the full support and cooperation of the United States government. Chief among these pesticides was a "miracle" formula called Dichloro-Diphenyl-Trichloroethane, or DDT. This pesticide was widely used during the war to kill pests that affect troops, such as lice and mosquitoes. After the war, use of DDT expanded to the home front. Farmers used DDT to kill pests that ate crops. Towns used it to kill mosquitoes that carried disease. Most people considered these chemicals a huge step forward in the battle against pests. Few could guess that there was a dangerous side to these pesticides.

few birds seen anywhere were moribund; they trembled violently and could not fly. It was a spring without voices. On the mornings that had once throbbed with the dawn chorus of … scores of bird voices there was now no sound; only silence lay over the fields and woods and marsh.

Rachel's book hit the nation like a bombshell. There was a chorus of outrage. People called for Congress to do something about pesticide poisoning. The book was also a shock to the companies that made the pesticides. They violently attacked *Silent Spring* and its author. A *New York Times* headline from July 1962 showed just how heated the controversy had become. It read: "'Silent Spring' is Now Noisy Summer."

The June 1963 hearing gave Rachel an opportunity to address her critics and state her case. It was also an incredible opportunity to influence public policy. The author sat calmly at the table. She seemed to be unaware of the lights, the crowd, and the suppressed excitement in the room. A pile of large note cards was stacked neatly on the table in front of her. Rachel Carson had done her homework. She was ready to face any opposition. She was ready to persuade Congress to pass laws controlling the spraying of DDT and other dangerous chemicals.

Senator Ribicoff began the hearing by saying "Miss Carson … we welcome you here. You are the lady who started all of this. Will you please proceed."

The Mighty Pen

Senator Ribicoff's opening remark to Rachel Carson was similar to one made by President Abraham Lincoln when he met Harriet Beecher Stowe. Stowe's book *Uncle Tom's Cabin* was widely credited with influencing opinions about slavery in the years before the American Civil War (1861–1865). Ribicoff felt that *Silent Spring* was playing a similar role in the battle to preserve the environment.

Rachel was ready. She spoke in a low, precise voice. "The problem you have chosen to explore," she began, "is one that must be solved in our time. I feel strongly that a beginning must be made on it now—in this session of Congress." She then carefully laid out the case against the widespread use of pesticides. She cited example after example of death and destruction on land and in the sea caused by pesticides. In conclusion, she urged the Senate to pass laws that would put new controls on pesticide use.

"You are the lady who started all of this."

– SENATOR ABRAHAM RIBICOFF

THE BIRTH OF A MOVEMENT

Rachel's life revolved around three things: the search for truth through science, a love of nature, and a love of writing. She was a skilled writer and scientist, not a revolutionary. Yet she started a kind of revolution. Rachel's groundbreaking work gave rise to the modern environmental movement.

It is hard to imagine a time when people didn't recycle, or when it was acceptable to dump waste in rivers and streams. Today, it is hard to imagine that people didn't know—or care—how their actions affected the planet. This was the case, however, mere decades ago, until Rachel Carson's work on behalf of the environment became a catalyst for change.

Today, companies, individuals—even government officials—are judged by how "green" they are. Every year we celebrate Earth Day and hold concerts to benefit the planet. There's even a government agency dedicated to the protection of our

Former U.S. Vice President Al Gore, a strong admirer of Rachel Carson, took a group of children on a tour of Rachel's childhood homestead in 2000. Gore went on to win the 2007 Nobel Peace Prize for his efforts to save the environment.

world: The Environmental Protection Agency (EPA). Not coincidentally, that agency was formed as a result of the June 1963 hearings on environmental hazards.

All of these things are connected. And their roots all lead back to the seeds that were planted by Rachel in 1962. "*Silent Spring* came as a cry in the wilderness, a deeply felt, thoroughly researched, and brilliantly written argument that changed the course of history," wrote former Vice President Al Gore. "[Rachel

Carson] had awakened not only our nation but the world. The publication of *Silent Spring* can properly be seen as the beginning of the modern environmental movement."

Gore is not alone in his admiration for Rachel Carson. In 1999, *Time* magazine named her one of the 100 most influential people of the 20th century. "Carson was not a born crusader but an intelligent and dedicated woman who rose heroically to the occasion," said the editors at *Time*.

Rachel would have been surprised by all the accolades. Her goal in writing *Silent Spring* was not to game fame. She had a more important motive. As she wrote to a friend in 1962:

> "The publication of *Silent Spring* can properly be seen as the beginning of the modern environmental movement."
>
> – AL GORE

The beauty of the living world I was trying to save has always been uppermost in my mind—that, and anger at the senseless, brutish things that were being done. I have felt bound by a solemn obligation to do what I could—if I didn't at least try I could never be happy again in nature. But now I can believe that I have at least helped a little. It would be unrealistic to believe one book could bring a complete change.

Rachel might not have believed she could bring about complete change, but she did. It didn't happen overnight, but thanks to Rachel—and those that have followed in her footsteps—the dream of preserving the natural world is becoming a reality. ❖

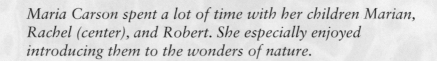

Maria Carson spent a lot of time with her children Marian, Rachel (center), and Robert. She especially enjoyed introducing them to the wonders of nature.

CHAPTER TWO

A CHILD OF SPRING

THE CHARACTERISTICS THAT BEST DEFINED Rachel Carson were her love of nature, her independent spirit, and her strong will. These were all gifts from her mother, Maria.

Maria, who was born in 1869, was just 11 years old when her father died. She was raised by her mother and aunts in Canonsburg, Pennsylvania, just outside of Pittsburgh. Maria's mother was a strong and independent woman, and she passed these traits on to her daughter. She also gave her daughter a love for learning and respect for education.

After high school, Maria attended Washington Female Seminary to continue her education. This was not a common choice for a young woman in the 19th century. After graduating in 1887 with honors in Latin and training in music, she taught school. To bring in extra money, Maria also gave piano lessons.

In 1893, Maria met a shy young man named Robert Carson. Born in 1864, Robert was the eldest of the six children of James and Ellen Carson, who had come to Pennsylvania from Ireland. Robert and Maria married in June 1894, and the young bride immediately gave up her job. In Pennsylvania at that time, married women were not allowed to teach. The couple, who would soon have many mouths to feed, would struggle financially for the rest of their married life.

In 1897, the Carsons welcomed a daughter, Marian, into the family. A son, Robert, followed barely two years later. The elder Robert's job as a traveling salesman for an insurance company did not pay well. Still, even though money was tight, the couple decided to purchase a home for their growing family.

A PLACE TO CALL HOME

On April 2, 1900, Robert took out a loan to buy about 65 acres (26 hectares) of land in Springdale, Pennsylvania. Springdale lay on the Allegheny River about 20 miles (32 kilometers) north of Pittsburgh. The property had a two-story house, a barn, a garage, and a chicken coop. It also had two outhouses. Indoor plumbing was very scarce in rural Pennsylvania in 1900.

The Carsons' main house was simply laid out. It had two small rooms—a living room and dining room—on the first floor. A central staircase led up to two small bedrooms on the second floor. The house did not have an indoor kitchen. Maria cooked the family's meals in a lean-to attached to the back of the house. She grew a large garden behind the garage. The Carsons used the cellar to store their fruits and vegetables.

Fittingly, when Rachel Louise Carson entered the world on May 27, 1907, nature was noisily alive. Insects were buzzing and birds were singing. Grass was growing and the trees were in leaf. The countryside held promise for a warm summer.

Maria was delighted with her newborn girl. She described Rachel as a "dear, plump, little blue-eyed baby, unusually pretty, and very good."

A MOTHER'S TOUCH

Robert Carson was a kind, quiet man. But the real center of family life at home, especially for Rachel, was Maria. She co-ordinated her children's activities and read to them often. She

By the time she was 5 years old, Rachel was already an avid reader. The little girl especially enjoyed reading to her dog Candy.

also made sure to take the children outdoors every day. One of Maria's great interests was the study of nature. The plants and animals that thrived along the Allegheny River fascinated her. Maria told her children stories about the birds, insects, and animals that shared their property. From the time Rachel was one year old, Maria spent increasing amounts of time outdoors with her. While Marian and Robert were at school, Maria and Rachel spent the day doing chores, singing, and going on nature walks.

> ### "I read a great deal almost from infancy."
> – RACHEL CARSON

Years later Rachel talked about those walks with her mother. She recalled how, as a young girl, she had responded to her mother's love of nature. She said her ability for precise observation, which made her an outstanding scientist, was shaped by these early walks. Rachel also said that, as a young child, she was "happiest with wild birds and creatures as companions." She would remain so all her life.

When Rachel was 6 years old, Maria enrolled her in Springdale grammar school. The little girl, who could already read, enjoyed school very much. But she was absent a lot. If there was any illness going around or if the weather was very cold, Maria kept Rachel home from school. She was not being overprotective. In those days, childhood diseases such as scarlet fever and diphtheria were widespread and sometimes fatal. Despite missing many days of school, Rachel was an A student.

As a child, Rachel had two great loves: nature and reading. "I read a great deal almost from infancy," she recalled later in life. Beatrix Potter's animal stories were Rachel's particular favorites.

Beatrix Potter

Beatrix Potter was born in South Kensington, London, in 1866. Educated at home, Potter had little opportunity to play with other children. She loved nature and her many pets, which included frogs, newts, and even a bat. She also had two rabbits: Benjamin and Peter. Potter would spend hours watching animals and sketching them. She made up stories about her animal friends and those she observed in the wild during family vacations. Potter, who influenced Rachel, is best known as the author of *The Tale of Peter Rabbit,* a favorite of young children all over the world. She eventually wrote 23 books, all published in a small format that were easy for children to hold and read.

The little girl also loved the adventures of Toad and Mole and their friends in *Wind in the Willows.*

A NEW DAY DAWNS

In 1917, the Carsons' peaceful world was shattered. The United States entered World War I (1914–1918). Robert joined the Army Air Service and went to Texas for training as a pilot. After that, he was shipped to Europe to fight the Germans in the skies above France. The Carsons worried about Robert constantly. They waited anxiously for each new letter from their son. Only then could they know a little peace.

One of Robert's letters had a different impact on Rachel's life. It led the young girl to take her first step toward becoming a published writer. Each month Rachel eagerly awaited the arrival of her *St. Nicholas Magazine,* and read it from cover to cover. One section of the magazine, the St. Nicholas League, was dedicated to publishing stories written by children. The League motto was "Live to learn and learn to live." Every month there were contests for the best writing, drawings, and puzzles submitted by children. Winners received gold badges and runners-up received silver badges. The contests were open to any child under the age of 18 years old.

Marian (left) and Rachel (right) were happy to see Robert return in 1919 after fighting in World War I.

St. Nicholas Magazine

St. Nicholas Magazine, published from 1873 to 1941, was designed for children from 5 to 18 years old. The editor was Mary Mapes Dodge, author of a popular children's book *Hans Brinker or the Silver Skates.* From the start, *St. Nicholas Magazine* published the work of the best illustrators and writers for children. Dodge wanted the magazine to provide gifts of fun as well as learning. She wanted it to be a "child's playground: where children could be delighted as well as be in charge." As with Rachel Carson, *St. Nicholas Magazine* published early works by such famous authors as Mark Twain, F. Scott Fitzgerald, Louisa May Alcott, and E. B. White.

Rachel was determined to submit a story to the League. As she tried to come up with an idea for her story, she remembered a letter that Robert had sent from France. Robert's letter about a brave Canadian pilot became the basis for Rachel's submission "A Battle in the Clouds." The story read, in part:

One day, when [the Canadian pilot] and one of his companions were flying, a German plane suddenly burst upon them from behind a cloud. The two planes began firing … For a while, neither plane was injured, but soon … a part of one wing of the Canadian aviator's plane had been shot away. The plane wavered, and he knew that if something was not done promptly, the plane would fall. He saw there was only one thing to do, and he did it quickly. He crawled out along the wing, inch by inch, until he reached the end. He then hung from the end of the wing, the weight making the plane balance properly.

Rachel submitted her story to *St. Nicholas* in May 1918. Then she waited nervously for the next issues of the magazine to arrive. Months passed. When the September issue of *St. Nicholas* arrived, Rachel opened it up and couldn't believe her eyes. Her story had been published! Even more exciting— right next to the title was printed "silver badge." "I doubt that any royalty check of recent years has given me as great joy as the notice of that award," she recalled many years later.

> **"I doubt that any royalty check of recent years has given me as great joy as the notice of that [St. Nicholas League] award."**
>
> – RACHEL CARSON

Rachel continued to submit stories to *St. Nicholas*. One even won a gold badge. By the end of 1919, she'd had four stories published. Rachel now knew for certain that she wanted to be a professional writer. But first she had to get through high school!

HIGH SCHOOL DAYS

Rachel finished eighth grade in 1921. Many of her classmates moved on to different high schools in the area. But Rachel stayed at her old school for the first two years of high school. For her junior and senior years Rachel traveled by streetcar to Parnassus

At the time of her high school graduation in 1925, Rachel looked forward to going to college and becoming a writer.

High School, a few miles away. She played on the high school's basketball and field hockey teams. Rachel was an excellent student, graduating first in her class of 28 girls and 16 boys.

Robert and Maria Carson took great pride in Rachel's accomplishments. She was the only one of their children to finish high school. Rachel was happy, but she looked forward to going on to college. Maria had passed on an important gift to her daughter: the desire to use her mind and pursue a meaningful career. Rachel wanted a college degree, and she wanted to be a writer. These were things that very few men—and even fewer women—of the time had the desire or ability to achieve. ❖

Rachel's mother and father visited her frequently at the Pennsylvania College for Women.

CHAPTER THREE

COLLEGE BOUND

B Y THE SUMMER OF 1925, RACHEL WAS ANXIOUS to leap into higher education. The Pennsylvania College for Women (PCW) was in Pittsburgh, only 16 miles (26 km) from Springdale. Maria was sure it was right for her daughter. Rachel won admission easily, but that was only half the battle. Tuition cost $1,000 per year. The Carsons struggled to put food on the table. Where would they find the tuition money?

PCW awarded Rachel a $100 scholarship based on her high school record. She also competed in an annual state scholarship examination and won another $100. To earn the additional $800, Robert put part of his land up for sale and Maria took in more piano students. The Carsons sold chickens and even the family china. But their efforts weren't enough. Luckily, PCW President Cora Coolidge was impressed with Rachel. She quietly arranged for payment of the rest of Rachel's college expenses.

A COLLEGE FOR WOMEN

Rachel arrived at PCW in September 1925. She quickly became friends with her roommate, Dorothy Appleby. Aside from this friendship, though, Rachel never really became "one of the girls." This pattern would repeat itself throughout her school years.

Rachel was reserved and independent. Her close family ties might have also kept her from having a more active social life at PCW. Maria came to visit her daughter almost every weekend. On those weekends that Maria didn't visit the campus, Rachel took the train home to Springdale. In addition to offering her daughter companionship, Maria also provided a valuable service to Rachel. She typed most of her papers. This arrangement would last well into Rachel's career as a professional writer.

Although she was serious about her studies, Rachel did take part in some aspects of non-classroom college life. She went out for the basketball team—even though she was only 5'4". She also joined the college field hockey team.

A teammate called Rachel (top row, second from right) a whiz at field hockey. She said that Rachel "seldom let a puck past her."

CHARTING HER COURSE

Rachel hoped to become a professional writer, so she majored in English at PCW. She was encouraged in her ambition by Grace Croff, who taught freshman composition. From what she could see of Rachel's work, Professor Croff thought she had great promise as a writer. By the end of her freshman year, Rachel had written three pieces that Croff particularly liked. One was a short story that Rachel submitted for a term paper. It was set along the New England seacoast and was entitled "The Master of the Ship's Light." The story had vividly accurate descriptions of the seacoast and the sea.

What's remarkable about "The Master of the Ship's Light" is that Rachel had never even been near the sea! She was able to paint a convincing picture just using her imagination and the knowledge she'd gained from years of reading about the ocean.

When Rachel returned home for the summer after her freshman year, the house was in chaos. Her sister, Marian, had left her husband and was living at home with her two daughters. Rachel's brother, Robert, also lived there with his wife. Robert's marriage was falling apart, too. The house was often filled with the sound of adults arguing and children crying.

As always, Rachel found peace in the woods around her home. She took long hikes along the hills above the Allegheny River. She read and wrote poetry. Most of all, though, she looked forward to the upcoming fall semester. Rachel had registered for another writing class with Croff. She also signed up for a beginning biology class. Rachel had no way of knowing it, but that one small decision would radically change the course of her life.

English professor Grace Croff (left) was very impressed with Rachel's writing ability and encouraged her to go on to a writing career.

THE PATH TO THE SEA

Mary Scott Skinker taught the beginning biology class. Skinker was immediately impressed by Rachel. The young woman worked hard. She also seemed to have an incredible depth of knowledge about the natural world. Rachel was equally impressed by her teacher. Skinker followed up classroom and lab work with trips to fields, streams, and wetlands around the area. Rachel enjoyed these trips as grown-up versions of the walks she used to take with her mother. Years later, Rachel said that her introduction to biology presented her with a deeply satisfying way of coming to terms with the mystery and meaning of life.

Rachel's newfound love of science presented her with a problem. Suddenly she wasn't sure whether she was meant to be a writer or a scientist.

One winter night, as a violent thunderstorm raged outside, Rachel sat reading a poem by Alfred, Lord Tennyson, titled "Locksley Hall." As the building shook around her, Rachel read "For the mighty wind arises, roaring seaward, and I go."

"That line spoke to something within me," Rachel later wrote, "seeming to tell me that my own path led to the sea … and that my own destiny was somehow linked with the sea." That was an odd feeling for a young woman who had never even seen the sea. Yet, it helped her come to a decision. She would continue to major in English and would minor in science.

> **"That [Tennyson] line spoke to something within me, seeming to tell me that my own path led to the sea … and that my own destiny was somehow linked with the sea."**
>
> – RACHEL CARSON

Under Skinker's direction, Rachel found herself more and more drawn to biology. She wanted to see deeply into the natural world, to discover how life worked. She was growing confused about her decision to stick with a major in English. By her junior year, she found herself moving toward a career in science.

The very thought of pursuing this path instead of becoming a writer was frightening. In the 1920s, writing was an acceptable profession for a woman. Science was another matter. There were very few women in the field, either in teaching or in research. Rachel knew that if she decided on a career in science, it would be difficult to find a good job. Even if she did manage to find a job, she would be faced with prejudice that would make it difficult to succeed. Rachel was not one to shrink from taking a difficult path in life, however.

In January 1928, Rachel changed her major to biology. By spring, she was sure she had made the right decision. When Rachel returned from spring break, however, she received unsettling news. Skinker was leaving PCW to continue her own education at Johns Hopkins University in Baltimore, Maryland.

Rachel decided to follow her mentor to Johns Hopkins. In April, she applied for graduate standing in zoology at the university. Rachel was accepted on May 8. Unfortunately, she couldn't afford the tuition. She had no choice but to remain at PCW for her senior year. Then she could try again, in hopes of getting a scholarship.

Rachel's Calling

Zoology is the study of animal life, from the simplest single-cell organisms to complex animals such as whales. Zoology and botany, the study of plant life, make up biology, the study of all living things. Rachel was interested in all life, including plants, and how both plants and animals interacted. But she was particularly interested in animal life. That's why she chose zoology as a field of study at Johns Hopkins.

When Rachel graduated from PCW in June 1928 she was at the top of her class. The entire Carson family was there for the graduation ceremony.

Rachel reapplied to Johns Hopkins in December, and quickly gained admission to the zoology department. The university also awarded her a full scholarship for her first year of graduate work. This was very welcome news. Rachel still owed $1,600 in tuition to PCW.

When Rachel graduated from PCW on June 10, she was one of three students to graduate *magna cum laude*—at the top of her class. The entire Carson family was on hand to see the ceremony. It was a proud moment for Rachel. But in her mind, she had already moved on to her next adventure. At the end of the summer, Rachel would be spending six weeks in an internship at the Marine Biological Laboratory (MBL) at Woods Hole, Massachusetts. Professor Skinker had arranged it all. Rachel was finally going "seaward" and taking the first step toward realizing her dream of becoming a scientist. ❖

Rachel was happy to spend part of the summer of 1928
at the Marine Biological Laboratory at Woods Hole.
It was a dream come true for her to be at sea, studying
nature and preparing for a career in biology.

CHAPTER FOUR

ADVENTURES IN BIOLOGY

RACHEL SPENT THE FIRST PART OF THE SUMMER at home in Springdale. She walked in the woods surrounding the house and followed the little streams that fed into the Allegheny River. But for the first time in her life, these nature walks did not bring Rachel peace.

The land had changed while Rachel was away at college—especially the river. Runoff from power plants located farther up the Allegheny had polluted the water. The contamination was made worse by heavy boat traffic on the river. Rachel was disgusted by what this pollution had done to the environment. She was worried about the health and safety of both the plants and animals that lived in the area.

Rachel's summer internship at Woods Hole would take her farther from her mother than ever before. But by mid-July, Rachel was ready—even anxious—to board the train for New

York City. From there, she would board a boat headed for Massachusetts and Woods Hole. This was quite an adventure for a young woman who had never been farther than 16 miles (26 km) from home in her life!

SEAWARD

After boarding the boat, Rachel settled herself into her tiny cabin and hurried up to the deck. She was "at sea" for the first time in her life. She didn't want to miss a minute. Rachel could barely contain her excitement at the thought of reaching Woods Hole. When she finally reached her destination, she was not disappointed. Woods Hole was just as she had imagined it.

The large headquarters of the U.S. Fish Commission dominated the small seaside community. The Commission had chosen Woods Hole for its field laboratory in 1871. A field laboratory is a lab that is set up in the habitat of the objects to be studied. The wide variety of marine habitats at Woods Hole made it an ideal spot in which to conduct research.

"I spent hours searching for the questions to answers that filled my mind."

– RACHEL CARSON

In 1888, a separate unit, the Marine Biological Laboratory (MBL), was also set up at Woods Hole to further the knowledge of marine biology. (Marine biology is the scientific study of the animals that live in the sea.) Young researchers such as Rachel were given summer internships at the MBL to boost their careers.

Rachel shared a room at Woods Hole with Mary Frye, a friend from PCW. The girls were delighted with their beginning marine zoology class. They finally had the chance to actually experiment on live specimens of sea urchins, horseshoe crabs, and other creatures. Rachel was also thrilled by the opportunity to study in the MBL's huge library—a place that she found magical. Here, in one place, Rachel had access to scientific journals from around the world, as well as new books about the sea. It was at Woods Hole, Rachel later wrote, that she "began storing away facts about the sea." Rachel gathered these facts by dissecting sea creatures and spending many hours in MBL's library "searching for the answers to questions that filled my mind," she said.

Rachel did not spend all her time in the laboratory and library, though. She and Mary also liked to walk along the ocean

Woods Hole—a quiet community by the sea—has played a major role in the development of marine biology since 1871.

shore at low tide when the retreating water exposed a wide variety of life. Rachel, especially, was enchanted with the sounds and smells of the ocean. She felt that it was here, at the edge of the sea, that the timeless ancient rhythms of the universe came to life. Rachel would remember this experience of seeing the ocean shore and its life forms all of her life.

"Each time I enter [the shore] I gain some new awareness of its beauty and its deeper meanings, sensing the intricate fabric of life by which one creature is linked with another, and each with its surroundings."

– RACHEL CARSON

The multitude of life Rachel found along the shore at Woods Hole made a lasting impression. So did the shore's fragile nature and each being's dependence on every other being. Rachel ultimately put her feelings into words in her book *The Edge of the Sea*. "Each time I enter it," she wrote about the shore, "I gain some new awareness of its beauty and its deeper meanings, sensing the intricate fabric of life by which one creature is linked with another, and each with its surroundings."

Rachel's six-week internship sped by. At the end of September 1929, she was ready to report for classes at Johns Hopkins. Before traveling to Baltimore, however, she took a quick trip to Washington, D.C. At the suggestion of Skinker, Rachel was meeting with Elmer Higgins. Higgins was the acting director of the U.S. Bureau of Fisheries. Skinker thought that he would be able to advise Rachel about job opportunities. Higgins told Rachel that her best chance of getting work in biology was a job

The Great Depression

The hard times experienced by the Carson family in the early 1930s were shared by millions of Americans. The Great Depression was the longest and most severe economic downturn in American history. It began in 1929 with the collapse of the New York Stock Market and lasted until 1939. By 1933, nearly half of all United States banks had failed. The money people had deposited in those banks was gone—as if it had simply disappeared. Millions of people went hungry and were made homeless.

with the government. But he warned her that it would not be easy. All of the biologist jobs in his department, except for one, were held by men.

As it turns out, events just on the horizon would make it difficult for anyone to land a job—in any field. Just a few weeks after Rachel's meeting with Higgins, the stock market collapsed. The United States entered the Great Depression (1929–1939). Eventually, 16 million Americans would find themselves out of work as businesses around the country—and the world—failed.

Rachel had already started her coursework at Johns Hopkins when the Depression hit. As economic conditions worsened, the Carsons decided to combine resources. The rest of the family joined Rachel in Maryland. Rachel found a home in Stemmers Run, a rural community about 13 miles (21 km) from Baltimore.

The house was quite a bit larger than the one in Springdale—and it had indoor plumbing! Rachel's parents moved into the new house in the spring of 1930. Marian and her daughters, Virginia and Marjorie, arrived in June. Rachel's brother Robert remained in Springdale trying to rent the old house.

A "SPLENDID" EXPERIENCE

Rachel was generally happy at Johns Hopkins. (Despite the fact that out of more than 80 graduate students in biology and botany, only 23 were women.) "The professors are splendid to work with," Rachel wrote to her friend Mary Frye.

Rachel found her coursework at Johns Hopkins challenging. The 22-year-old student worked hard to get the most out of the experience.

All the zoology courses at Johns Hopkins emphasized laboratory work, which Rachel often found boring. She preferred to be out in the field. In her first year, Rachel took four courses each semester. The most challenging, by far, was organic chemistry. When she scored an 85 on an exam, the A student wrote to Mary Frye: "I was never so proud of an 85 in my life!"

Rachel was glad to survive the first year of graduate study. She looked forward to finding a job during the summer months. An opportunity came up almost immediately. Rachel had made friends with Grace Lippy, who taught an undergraduate zoology course at Johns Hopkins during

> **"I was never so proud of an 85 in my life!"**
>
> – RACHEL CARSON

the summer. Lippy knew that Rachel needed a job, so she hired her as a laboratory assistant. Rachel's job was to wash and lay out equipment for Lippy's students. She also helped them with their experiments. Lippy conducted the lectures, and Rachel designed and coordinated the lab experiments.

The two women worked well together. In fact, Lippy was the only friend Rachel made during her three years in graduate school. They would continue to teach summer school together for the next four years.

Rachel had already decided that she wanted to get a doctorate degree after she finished her masters program. After that, she hoped to go on to a teaching career. But in Rachel's second year of graduate studies, fate stepped in. She had obtained a full-tuition scholarship for her first year of graduate study. Now there was an increase in tuition costs that her scholarship did not

Johns Hopkins University

Johns Hopkins University is named after Johns Hopkins (1795–1873). The wealthy Maryland businessman left $7 million in his will to found a hospital and university. At the time it was the largest philanthropic bequest in United States history. (It is roughly equivalent to $131 million in today's dollars.) The university quickly became a top American institution, especially in scientific research. Today, as in Rachel Carson's day, Johns Hopkins leads the country in money spent for science, medical, and engineering research.

Rachel attended graduate school at Johns Hopkins in Baltimore, Maryland. Gilman Hall (above) was the university's main academic building during the early 20th century.

completely cover. The only way Rachel could afford the tuition was if she got a part-time job during the school year. Unfortunately, that meant she'd have to cut back on classes and become a part-time student. Rachel wrote to all the campus departments and the Johns Hopkins medical school asking for a job. She was hired to work as a lab assistant at the Institute for Biological Research in the School of Hygiene and Public Health.

Despite her new job, Rachel still had serious money problems. In addition to her Johns Hopkins tuition, Rachel had to pay back PCW. And she was the main support for her family. In February 1930, Rachel sent a letter to PCW, which read in part:

> *To tell of the difficulties which the widespread depression and unemployment have brought to our household would be only to repeat the story which you are hearing on all sides, I am sure. However, the combination of circumstances has been a little more than I could cope with. ... As a result, we have been so heavily dependent upon my earnings for the bare necessities of living that there was just nothing to send you last month, and I am sorry to say that for the next month or so at least I can see no better prospects.*

In the end, Rachel was forced to give PCW much of her family's land in Springdale as payment for the debt. Her brother Robert and his family joined the rest of the Carsons in Baltimore in 1931. He got a job in a radio repair shop, and so was able to help out a little. Unfortunately, Robert's boss could not always afford to pay him.

Rachel continued her summer work with Grace Lippy. During the school year, she worked at a new job as a biology instructor at the Dental and Pharmacy School of the University of Maryland. Though the new job helped keep Rachel in school, it also took time away from her studies. She found that she could not keep up with the other students and also do her job.

In order to earn her master's degree, Rachel, like all graduate students, had to complete a thesis, or long research paper. She finally completed her thesis in the spring of 1932 and passed her oral examination in May. It had taken Rachel one year longer than she'd planned, but on June 14, 1932, she was awarded her master's degree.

After earning her master's degree, Rachel tried to make extra money by writing.

A DREAM DEFERRED

Rachel began the doctorate program at Johns Hopkins in September 1932. Unfortunately, she would not get very far in her studies. Things were not going well at home. Rachel's sister Marian was sickly and very often unable to work. Rachel's father also suffered from poor health. Once again, it was up to Rachel to shoulder the responsibility for the rest of her family. By the fall of 1933, Rachel was the only one in the family able to earn any income. At the start of the 1934 spring semester she was forced to drop out of the doctorate program and go to work full time.

Rachel looked for a teaching position, but without success. In desperation, she revised poems and short stories that she had written in college and submitted them to magazines. No one was interested in publishing her work.

On July 6, 1935, Rachel's father came into the kitchen and told Maria that he felt ill. He went out the back door and fell forward onto the grass. Maria ran outside and gathered her husband in her arms, but there was nothing she could do. Robert died at age 71, cradled in his wife's arms. The family shipped Robert's body to his sisters in Pennsylvania for burial. His wife and children did not attend the funeral. There was no money for the trip. ❖

Rachel was happy to find work with the U.S. Bureau of Fisheries during the Great Depression.

CHAPTER FIVE

REDISCOVERING WRITING

T HE YEAR 1935 MARKED A TERRIBLE TIME IN history. The storm clouds of war were gathering in Europe and Asia, as Nazi Germany and Japan set their sites on neighboring countries. Closer to home, millions of Americans struggled to fend off poverty and even starvation.

Robert Carson's death left little hope that Rachel would have any help keeping her family afloat. She was desperate to get a paying job. Once again, Rachel turned to her mentor for help. Mary Skinker advised Rachel to take the federal civil service examinations in several areas related to zoology. Then, if an opening appeared for a government job, Rachel would be able to apply for it. She would be one step ahead of those applicants who hadn't yet taken the exam.

Not surprisingly, Rachel did well on the examinations. She was that much closer to getting a job, but she still had to wait for an opening. Skinker urged Rachel to meet with Elmer Higgins again. Higgins had been promoted. He was now the division chief of the Bureau of Fisheries.

Higgins remembered Rachel from their first meeting and greeted her warmly. Unfortunately, there were no job openings in his department. But he did think there was a way he and Rachel could help each other out.

Higgins told Rachel about a "problem assignment" he'd been given by his superiors. The Bureau was supposed to produce a series of 52 short radio programs on marine life. Unfortunately, none of Higgins's biologists could write well. They couldn't put their knowledge into language that the general public found interesting. Higgins needed someone who knew biology but could also write well. Though he had never seen any of Rachel's writings, Higgins had a hunch she might be right for the job. "I've never seen a written word of yours," he told Rachel, "but I'm going to take a sporting chance."

U.S. Bureau of Fisheries

The U.S. Bureau of Fisheries began in 1871 as the U.S. Commission of Fish and Fisheries. In 1940, it acquired its present name: the U.S. Fish and Wildlife Service. Today, the Fish and Wildlife Service is responsible for enforcing federal wildlife laws, maintaining fisheries, and protecting endangered species.

Years later, Rachel described this moment as a turning point in her life. Rachel thought she "had given up writing forever" when she switched majors from English to biology. "It never occurred to me," she later wrote "that I was merely getting something to write about."

For the next eight months, Rachel rode the bus to Washington, D.C., two days a week and wrote radio scripts for the *Romance Under the Waters* series. She was paid $6.50 a day.

> **"I've never seen a written word of yours, but I'm going to take a sporting chance."**
>
> – ELMER HIGGINS

Rachel's job enabled her to keep food on the table. The Carsons were out of the woods for a while, at least.

The weekly radio broadcasts were a success. Everyone at the Bureau was pleased with what Rachel wrote. In fact, Rachel did so well that when she finished the 52 scripts, Higgins gave her another assignment. He asked her to write a general introduction to marine life for a government brochure.

THE WORLD OF WATERS

Rachel immediately began work on the essay, which she titled "The World of Waters." In the meantime, she also sent off an article on the decline of a local fishery to the *Baltimore Sun*. The newspaper paid Rachel $20 for the story—the equivalent of almost two weeks' pay. It appeared in the March 1 Sunday magazine section under the byline of R. L. Carson.

Rachel had been using this pen name of sorts from the time she started working on *Romance under the Waters*. She and

Rachel was perhaps the most famous employee of the U.S. Bureau of Fisheries. The Bureau named one of its research vessels in her honor.

others thought that she would be taken more seriously if readers thought she was a man. At the time, not many women were writing about science subjects.

Rachel hand-delivered "The World of Waters" to Higgins. Then she sat quietly in his crowded office while he read. She waited nervously for his reaction. Higgins finished reading Rachel's piece and handed back the manuscript. "I don't think it will do," is all he said. Rachel felt a moment of panic before she noticed a twinkle in his eye. "Better try again," he continued. "But send this one to the *Atlantic!*"

Higgins thought that Rachel's writing was actually too good for a government brochure. He felt the essay was better suited to *The Atlantic Monthly,* a prized literary magazine of the time. Rachel was utterly surprised and delighted. She put the essay away for later publication and wrote a much simpler version for the brochure.

The Atlantic Monthly

Having an article published in *The Atlantic Monthly* in the 1930s and '40s meant you had made it as a writer. It was one of the oldest and most respected magazines in America. In addition to Rachel Carson, *The Atlantic Monthly* published works by a number of famous writers, including Ralph Waldo Emerson, Henry Wadsworth Longfellow, and Harriet Beecher Stowe.

AN OFFICIAL APPOINTMENT

On July 6, 1936, Rachel was recommended for a full-time position as a junior aquatic biologist. She was officially appointed to the Bureau of Fisheries just one month later. Rachel's salary was $2,000 a year—a generous $38.48 per week! Her job was to analyze the marine life in Chesapeake Bay and to write and edit scientific reports about it. It was a dream job. At the time, Rachel was one of only two women who worked at the bureau in a non-secretarial role.

> "We have everyone of us been impressed by your uncommonly eloquent little essay."
>
> – EDWARD WEEKS

As often happened in Rachel's life, tragedy followed triumph. In January 1937, Rachel's sister Marian died of pneumonia. She was only 40 years old. Marian's two daughters, Virginia and Marjorie, ages 12 and 11, were left in Maria and Rachel's care.

Rachel's new job and family responsibilities demanded a lot of her time. But she continued to write articles for newspapers and magazines. Between January and June 1937, she published seven articles on Chesapeake Bay marine life. She also pulled out her "The World of Waters" essay, revised it, and submitted it to *The Atlantic Monthly*.

Edward Weeks, acting editor at the *Atlantic,* wrote to Rachel immediately after receiving her submission. "We have everyone of us been impressed by your uncommonly eloquent little essay," he wrote in the letter in which he offered to publish the piece. The essay, which had been re-titled "Undersea," ran in the September 1937 issue.

The essay bore the marks of Rachel's developing style. She had a remarkable talent for explaining complex scientific concepts in terms that the average reader could understand and be moved by. At the beginning of "Undersea," Rachel wrote:

Who has known the ocean? Neither you nor I, with our earth-bound senses, know the foam and surge of the tide that beats over the crab hiding under the seaweed of his tide-pool home; or the lilt of the long, slow swells of mid-ocean, where shoals of wandering fish prey and are preyed upon, and the dolphin breaks the waves to breathe the upper atmosphere.

After Rachel's older sister Marian died of pneumonia, her two daughters, Virginia (left) and Marjorie (right), were left in Rachel's care.

A NEW WORLD OPENS UP

The *Atlantic* article was only four pages long, but it almost instantly opened up a whole new world for Rachel. Hendrik van Loon, a well-known journalist and historian, praised the article in a letter to Rachel. Quincy Howe, a senior editor at Simon & Schuster, wrote to Rachel to ask if she would consider writing a book. Simon & Schuster was a big publishing house located in New York City.

At the beginning of 1938, Rachel met with Howe and van Loon to discuss a book about the sea. Howe was not ready to offer Rachel a contract, however. First, she had to show him several sample chapters.

In July 1938, Rachel took a 10-day trip to a beach near Beaufort, North Carolina. Her mother and nieces Virginia and Marjorie accompanied her. The four women spent many happy

Hendrik van Loon

Hendrik van Loon (1882–1944) was a historian and an illustrator famous for his children's books. He was the first recipient of the American Library Association's Newbery Medal. The Newbery Medal is given annually for excellence in children's literature. Van Loon won the medal for *The Story of Mankind,* an illustrated human history. His other best-selling works include *The Story of the Bible* (1923) and *Van Loon's Lives* (1942).

hours walking along the shore. Rachel especially delighted in showing her nieces the wonders that could be found at the edge of the sea.

Spending time at the beach with her mother and nieces brought Rachel great joy. She loved sharing her knowledge—and her world—with them. The experience itself was very moving for Rachel as well. Years later, Rachel recalled her intensely emotional response as she watched young fish who had been imprisoned in the tide pools race and jump to meet the clean cold water of the ocean. "I stood knee-deep in that racing water," she told a friend, "and at times could scarcely see those darting, silver bits of life for my tears."

> **"I stood knee-deep in that racing water, and at times could scarcely see those darting, silver bits of life for my tears."**
>
> – RACHEL CARSON

Rachel's experiences on that trip helped cement her emotions. She was able to more clearly focus her thoughts on the book that she was planning. In the early spring of 1940, Rachel submitted five chapters to Simon & Schuster. Howe and the other editors were impressed. It wasn't long before Rachel received a book contract and an advance check. Her career path had taken yet another turn. Rachel was about to become a book author. ❖

Rachel made several visits to Woods Hole after her first trip there in 1928. She often took notes that were later incorporated into her books about the sea.

CHAPTER SIX

A Different Kind of Book

DURING THE NEXT FEW YEARS, RACHEL WORKED on the book, titled *Under the Sea-Wind*. She usually worked alone in an upstairs bedroom early in the morning or late at night. That's when the house was quietest. Rachel's only companions were her two cats, Buzzie and Kito.

Rachel wanted to write a different kind of book about nature. She believed that most nature books were written from the viewpoint of people. Rachel wanted to write a book that, she said, avoided this "human bias" as much as possible.

Rachel always wrote her first drafts by hand. Every once in a while she would stop and read her words aloud to hear the sound and rhythm of her writing. Then she would rewrite again and again until the words sounded exactly as she wanted. Only then would she move onto the next sentence or paragraph. While Rachel was at work, Maria typed up what her daughter had written the night before. *Under the Sea-Wind* was published on November 1, 1941. Copies sold for $3 each.

The main character of the book is the ocean. Rachel tried to convey the feel of the ocean waters, the pounding of the waves—even the smell of the sea—on every page. *Under the Sea-Wind* is divided into three sections. Part one focuses on the life of the shore. Part two covers the open sea with its vast winds. Part three introduces the reader to the great depths of the ocean. Each section also features the range of creatures that populates each habitat.

Rachel wrote the first draft of Under the Sea-Wind by hand. Her mother later typed it up.

Critics loved the book. *The New York Times* found it "so skillfully written as to read like fiction, but in fact a scientifically accurate account of life in the ocean and along the ocean shore." Rachel's description of a black skimmer seabird in part one shows the style that inspired so much praise:

With the dusk a strange bird came to the island from its nesting grounds on the outer banks. Its wings were pure black, and from tip to tip their spread was more than the length of a man's arm. It flew steadily and without haste across the sound, its progress as measured and as meaningful as that of the shadows which little by little were dulling the bright water path. The bird was called Rynchops, the black skimmer.

As he neared the shore of the island the skimmer drifted closer to the water, bringing his dark form into strong silhouette against the gray sheet, like the shadow of a great bird that passed unseen above. Yet so quietly did he approach that the sound of his wings, if sound there were, was lost in the whisper song of the water turning over the shells on the wet sand.

Unfortunately, very few people bought *Under the Sea-Wind*. Only 2,000 copies were sold. World events had overcome interest in the sea and its life. On December 8, 1941, a little more than a month after Rachel's book was published, the United States was at war.

Pearl Harbor

World War II (1939–1945) had been raging in Europe for two years before the United States entered the fight. The war began for the United States when Japanese forces attacked the U.S. naval base at Pearl Harbor, Hawaii, on December 7, 1941. The attack occurred at 7:55 on a Sunday morning and lasted less than two hours. In that time, 21 American ships were sunk or damaged, 188 aircraft were destroyed, and 159 were damaged. More than 2,000 Americans were killed, including 68 civilians. One day later, the United States declared war on Japan.

RISING THROUGH THE RANKS

As America prepared for war, the federal government mush-roomed in size. At the end of May 1942, Rachel received a promotion. She was now an assistant aquatic biologist. Even though her title said biologist, she was really in charge of reviewing and editing reports and manuscripts. In 1943, she was promoted again to associate aquatic biologist, with pretty much the same responsibilities. Even though she was making her way up the ranks in the government, Rachel was dissatisfied. She felt that she was not fulfilling her life's purpose. In a letter, she described herself as a "would-be writer who could not afford the time for creative work."

In her official position, Rachel was in daily contact with biologists that were investigating methods of pest control. She was

Rachel greatly enjoyed her field work for the Bureau of Fisheries. She especially loved her work on Conservation in Action, *which allowed her to visit nature areas around the country, including the Chesapeake Bay.*

alarmed by some early test results of the new pesticide Dichloro-Diphenyl-Trichloroethane (DDT). It seemed that DDT had the potential to kill more than pests. It also seemed to spread poison throughout the food chain. In 1945, Rachel proposed an article about the dangers of DDT to *Reader's Digest,* but the magazine wasn't interested.

Things began to look up for Rachel in March 1946, when Albert M. Day became director of the Fish and Wildlife Service. Day quickly approved Rachel's plan for a new series of 12 booklets to be titled *Conservation in Action.* The series was designed to promote the agency's efforts to conserve natural resources in protected national wildlife refuges. Throughout much of 1946 and 1947, Rachel took a series of trips to refuges from North Carolina to Montana to the Columbia River in the northwest. She closely observed the wildlife and took careful notes. She also saw firsthand the intricate workings of nature and the interdependence of each living thing upon other living things. The two and a half years Rachel worked on the *Conservation in Action* series was her happiest time in the service.

At the end of June 1946, Rachel rented a house in Maine. She and her mother spent four happy weeks in the cozy cottage, which was surrounded by trees and close to the sea. It was the perfect escape for the two nature lovers. Rachel particularly enjoyed her walks along the shore, where she watched the sea creatures hiding under seaweed or clinging to the undersides of rocks during low tide. Rachel loved her time in Maine and vowed to live there one day, when—and if—she could make her living as a professional writer.

In 1966, the Rachel Carson National Wildlife Refuge was established in Maine. The land was set aside to protect salt marshes and estuaries for migratory birds.

Back in Washington D.C., Rachel was kept very busy at work. Yet she was determined to write another book. Although she kept gathering material, Rachel began to worry that the book might just be a pipe dream. Then she met Marie Rodell.

A MEETING OF THE MINDS

Marie Rodell was a mystery writer who had published three novels. In 1948, she decided to go into business as a literary agent. Literary agents connect authors with publishers. They also help authors shape books to appeal to editors. Although the two women were very different, they hit it off right away. Rachel mentioned to Rodell that she was working on a book about the sea, particularly its geography, history, composition, and life forms. Rodell was interested and pressed the author for a sample chapter and outline. When Rachel had one-third of the book written, Rodell sent it out to publishers for comment. Rachel's dream was becoming a reality. Oxford University Press agreed to publish the book.

In early July 1948, Rachel was happily working on her second book. There was just one thing bothering her. She was writing another book about the sea, but she had never actually been under the sea. Rachel contacted William Beebe, of the Miami Marine Laboratory, and asked for his help. Hendrik van Loon had introduced Rachel to Beebe in 1938, and the two had become friends. Beebe promised that if Rachel came to see him in Miami, he'd give her an undersea experience she would never forget.

No Girls Allowed

In 1949, Rachel (right) and Marie Rodell became the first women ever to sail as part of the scientific party aboard a federal fishery research vessel. From July 27 through August 5, Rachel and Marie participated in a Bureau of Commercial Fisheries cruise. At first, the men involved with the trip tried to cancel the cruise to prevent the women from participating.

Within days, Rachel was on her way to the Miami Marine Laboratory. She was thrilled to finally get the chance to go beneath the waves and observe the life of the undersea world. Rachel put on a heavy diving helmet and attached weights to her feet. Then she climbed down the ladder into the ocean water. She was delighted with what she saw. "How exquisitely delicate and varied [are] the colors displayed by the animals of the reef," she later wrote. "I got the feeling of the misty green vistas of a strange, nonhuman world."

William Beebe

Charles William Beebe was a biologist and a writer on natural history. Like Rachel, he combined careful research with good writing. In the 1930s, Beebe teamed up with inventor Otis Barton to create the bathysphere. The large iron sphere could be lowered to great depths in the ocean, allowing those inside to observe undersea life. Before this invention, people could only descend to 525 feet (160 meters). The bathysphere was made of one-inch thick steel. It had windows made of fused quartz, the strongest transparent material then available. On June 6, 1930, Beebe and Barton descended together to a depth of 600 feet (183 m) into the ocean. On August 15, 1934, the two made a world record descent to a depth of 3,028 feet (923 m). The record remained unbroken until 1947.

In 1948, with help from her friend William Beebe, Rachel prepared to put on a diving helmet and go under the waves for the first time.

Once again, Rachel would be juggling two jobs. After a full day at work, she would come home and write into the small hours of the night. As she prepared to return home from Miami, Rachel thought about the fact that something had to give. There just wasn't enough time to work on the book and hold her full-time job. Then Rachel's mother called with good news. Rachel had won the Saxton Fellowship. The award for little recognized writers came with a cash prize of $2,250. The money would allow Rachel to take several months off from work to complete the manuscript. ❖

Rachel was most comfortable writing her manuscripts by hand. Then she revised and rewrote the text before sending a typed manuscript to the publisher.

CHAPTER SEVEN

SEAS OF FORTUNE

E VEN WITH THE TIME OFF FROM WORK, BY MID-
February 1950, Rachel was racing to finish the new book.
As she worked, word began to spread about *The Sea
Around Us*. William Shawn, the editor of *The New Yorker*, was
a long-time fan of Rachel's work. He was familiar with *Under
the Sea-Wind* and the magazine and newspaper articles that she
had written. Now he hoped to publish one chapter of the new
book as soon as it was finished. *The New Yorker* was considered
the top literary magazine in the country. Being featured in its
pages would boost sales of *The Sea Around Us* beyond Rachel's
imagination.

Rachel's mother finished typing the final manuscript at
the beginning of July 1950. The writer felt tremendous relief
as she mailed the pages to the publisher. A huge burden had
been lifted off her shoulders. A new worry would soon take its

place, however. In September, Rachel checked into the hospital. Doctors had found a tumor in her breast. It would have to be removed. After the operation, Rachel asked if the tumor was a sign of cancer. The doctors said no. They told her that no further treatment was necessary.

PRAISE FOR HER NEW BOOK

Rachel's promising medical diagnosis was followed by more good news. *The Sea Around Us* began to gather praise even before it was published.

In December 1950, Rachel was awarded the Westinghouse Prize of $1,000 for "excellence in science writing." In March 1951 she was told that *The Sea Around Us* had been selected by the Book-of-the-Month Club (BMOC) for July or August.

The Book-of-the-Month Club

Harry Scherman started the original Book-of-the-Month Club (BOMC) in 1926. Scherman was an advertising executive who wanted to ensure that good books got the attention they deserved. Each month, people who belonged to the club received recommendations on the best books to buy. Then they could order the books right from the club. BMOC quickly became one of the most powerful institutions in the publishing world. In the 1950s, BMOC subscribers numbered in the millions.

Writing was Rachel's first love. But she combined it with a strong desire to find the truth through painstaking and extensive scientific research.

No happier news could have come her way. To have a book picked as the BMOC's monthly selection usually increased sales tremendously. That meant financial success for a writer. On June 3, 1951, Rachel asked for, and was given, a year's leave of absence from her job at the Fish and Wildlife Service. She was ready to start work on her next book.

Meanwhile, *The New Yorker* published a condensed version of *The Sea Around Us* in three parts, beginning on June 2. The book was released on July 2, 1951 to excellent reviews.

Critics weren't the only ones who loved *The Sea Around Us*. After only four months, the book had sold 100,000 copies. By the end of the year, it was selling at the rate of 4,000 books a day. *The Sea Around Us* remained on the *New York Times* Best Seller List for an extremely long time: 86 weeks.

In *The Sea Around Us,* Rachel described the great elemental forces that shaped the ocean and the world. And she did it in a way that even the most uninformed reader could understand and appreciate:

> *On land and sea the stream of life poured on. New forms evolved; some old ones declined and disappeared. On land the mosses and ferns and the seed plants developed. The reptiles for a time dominated the earth, gigantic, grotesque, and terrifying. Birds learned to live and move in the ocean of air. The first small mammals lurked inconspicuously in hidden crannies of the earth as though in fear of the reptiles.*

> *When they went ashore the animals that took up a land life carried with them a part of the sea in their bodies, a heritage which they passed on to their children and even*

Making The New York Times Best Seller List

Started in 1942, *The New York Times* Best Seller List is considered the most accurate list of best-selling books in the United States. It is still published weekly in *The New York Times Book Review* magazine, a section of the Sunday newspaper. The list is based on weekly sales reports from bookstores and other booksellers. The list is divided into fiction and nonfiction sections. Rachel Carson's book was included in the nonfiction section.

today links each land animal with its origin in the ancient sea … each of us carries in our veins a salty stream in which the elements sodium, potassium, and calcium are combined in almost the same proportions as in sea water …

The Sea Around Us was so popular that Oxford decided to buy the rights to republish Rachel's earlier book, *Under the Sea-Wind*. It was a wise choice. Critics, such as *The New York Times* book reviewer, were impressed. "Once or twice in a generation does the world get a physical scientist with literary genius," he wrote. "Miss Carson has written a classic in *The Sea Around Us. Under the Sea-Wind* may be another." Thousands of readers around the country agreed. Like *The Sea Around Us, Under the Sea-Wind* was a tremendous success.

> **"Once or twice in a generation does the world get a physical scientist with literary genius. Miss Carson has written a classic in *The Sea Around Us."***
>
> – NEW YORK TIMES CRITIC

SUDDEN FAME

Rachel Carson had become famous. She received fan letters from all over the world, and from people in all walks of life. She was invited to speak at functions all over the country. Women's groups, nature study groups, and literary groups all wanted to hear from the acclaimed author. Rachel turned most of the invitations down, however. She was naturally shy and believed that too

In 1952, Rachel received the National Book Award for nonfiction. Other winners included Marianne Moore for poetry and James Jones for fiction. Writer John Mason Brown (far right) presented the awards.

much touring and speaking would hurt her writing schedule. The acclaim was hard for Rachel to accept. "Heavens," she wrote to Marie Rodell, "is this all about me—it's really ridiculous!"

Rachel remained focused on her work. She continued to use her leave of absence from the Fish and Wildlife Service to research her next book. In May 1951, Rachel set off to explore the coastline from Maine to Florida. For the next several months, she and artist Bob Hines traveled up and down the eastern seaboard. They visited the Florida Keys to observe the life that abounded in the shore waters. They went to Maine to look at life along the rocky coasts.

Then, in January 1952, Rachel learned that she had won the National Book Award for nonfiction. Started in 1950, the National Book Awards are one of the top literary prizes in the United States. They are presented annually for literature published the prior year. On January 27, Rachel went to a special dinner in New York City to accept the award.

In her acceptance speech, Rachel explained why she had written *The Sea Around Us*. She spoke about her conviction that scientific knowledge belongs to everyone, not just a small group of scientists. She said:

> **"Heavens, is this all about me—it's really ridiculous!"**
>
> – RACHEL CARSON

Many people have commented with surprise on the fact that a work of science should have a large popular sale. But this notion that "science" is something that belongs ... apart from everyday life is one I should like to challenge. We live in a scientific age; yet we assume that knowledge of science [belongs to] only a small number of human beings. ... This is not true. It cannot be true. The materials of science are the materials of life itself. Science is part of the reality of living; it is the what, the how, and the why of everything ...

On April 7, 1952, Rachel received an honor that—for her—topped winning the National Book Award. She was awarded the John Burroughs Medal, which commemorates excellence in nature writing. The medal honored the great American naturalist

John Burroughs, a man Rachel revered. In accepting the medal, the writer said she felt an odd sense of unreality "in being linked … with the immortals in the field of nature writing." Rachel also touched on a theme that would occupy the latter years of her life:

> *Mankind has gone very far into an artificial world of his own creation. He has sought to insulate himself, in his cities of steel and concrete, from the realities of earth and water and the growing seed. Intoxicated with a sense of his own power, he seems to be going farther and farther into more experiments for the destruction of himself and his world.*

John Burroughs

John Burroughs (1837–1921) was a writer who dedicated his life to studying nature. After leaving his job as a clerk in the U.S. Treasury Department in 1873, he moved to a farm in New York's Hudson River Valley. For almost 50 years he wrote books and articles on nature subjects. His chief books include *Wake-Robin*, *Birds and Poets*, and *Ways of Nature*. His life and writing influenced many people, including Rachel Carson. The John Burroughs Association, a society that encourages nature writing, was established in his memory in 1921.

Artist Bob Hines traveled with Rachel up and down the Atlantic coast in order to draw specimens to illustrate The Edge of the Sea.

THE EDGE OF THE SEA

Rachel finished her research travels on the west coast of Florida. As she strolled along the beach watching the waves crash into the shore, Rachel came to a decision. It was time to realize her lifelong dream of being a full-time writer. On May 15, Rachel filled out and signed the Fish and Wildlife Service resignation forms. Her resignation became official on June 3, the day that her one-year leave of absence ended. Soon she was back in Maine, gathering more material for the book. She also started another project—building a summer home.

Over the course of her travels in 1952, Rachel had spotted a perfect spot on Maine's Southport Island to build a cottage. She bought land and hired a builder. By July 1953, Rachel, her

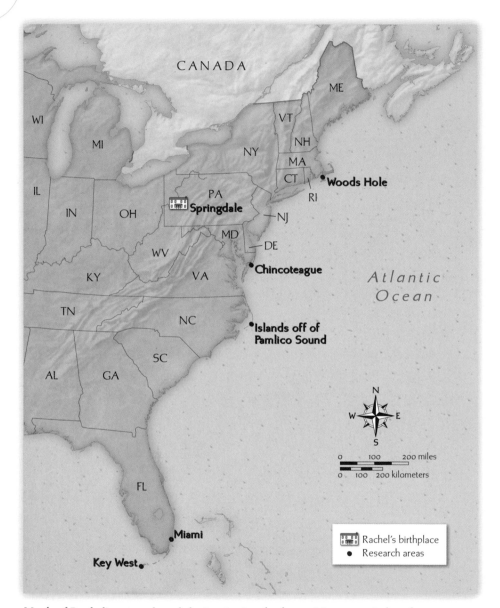

Much of Rachel's research and the inspiration for her writings was tied to the eastern seaboard of the United States. She traveled from Key West, Florida, to Maine to study the seacoast and to draw inspiration from the ebb and flow of the tides.

mother, and her cat were ready to move in. It was a great place to work. As she wrote, Rachel could hear the roar of the waves.

Rachel had conducted months of research for her new book. She originally planned it as a shoreline guide, with examples of the plants and animals that could be found on the Atlantic shore. Her research, however, indicated another approach. Rachel now saw the book as an explanation of the interdependence of life in three types of shores: rock, sand, and coral.

By the middle of March 1955, Rachel had turned in most of the manuscript to the publisher. Once again, the strain of writing a book wore her out. "It has been such a terribly long pull and I feel quite drained and exhausted," she wrote to fellow nature writer Edwin Teale.

Bob Hines

Robert W. Hines (1912–1994) was a highly regarded wildlife artist. He worked with Rachel to illustrate the *Conservation in Action* series for the Fish and Wildlife Service. He also joined Rachel to make a number of detailed drawings for *The Edge of the Sea*, Rachel's third book. His drawings and paintings are noted for their beauty, as well as for their scientific accuracy.

Once again, William Shawn wanted to serialize the new book in *The New Yorker* before it was published. *The Edge of the Sea* appeared in the magazine in two installments on August 20 and 27, 1955.

The book was published on October 26. By December, it had become a national best seller. Reviewers praised Rachel's ability to be both scientifically accurate and convey the poetry of nature

Rachel (right) and her niece Marjorie frequently explored the shore and the animals that lived in the tide pools.

and the sea. The first paragraph of the first chapter of the book, "The Marginal World" is one example of this skill:

After Marjorie died at age 31, Rachel adopted her son, Roger.

> *The edge of the sea is a strange and beautiful place. All through the long history of Earth it has been an area of unrest where waves have broken heavily against the land, where the tides have pressed forward over the continents, receded, and then returned. … Not only do the tides advance and retreat in their eternal rhythms, but the level of the sea itself is never at rest. It rises or falls as the glaciers melt or grow. … Today a little more land may belong to the sea, tomorrow a little less. Always the edge of the sea remains an elusive and indefinable boundary.*

Once again, with professional success came personal tragedy. Marjorie, Rachel's niece, developed pneumonia. On January 30, 1957, the single mom died, leaving behind her 5-year-old son Roger. Maria offered to take on most of the responsibility of caring for the boy. She was 88, however, and not physically up to the task. Instead, Rachel adopted Roger. Quite suddenly—at almost 50 years old—Rachel was a new mother. ❖

Rachel loved her summer cottage in Maine, which was close to both the woods and the ocean. She spent as much time as possible there.

CHAPTER EIGHT

THE WAR AGAINST NATURE

W ITH THE PUBLICATION OF HER THIRD BOOK in 1955, Rachel had every reason to be satisfied. She was a successful author, financially independent, and living where she wanted to live. But she was worried about what was happening to the natural world she loved so deeply. A lifetime of research had shown her that all of nature was interconnected. To Rachel, the world of living creatures formed an interlocking web. Each living thing is connected to and dependent on every other living thing. This was true, she believed, on land as well as in the sea.

As early as the late 1930s, Rachel had begun to see that humankind, with its blind faith in scientific progress, was unraveling nature's harmony. She saw chemicals developed to benefit people being dumped into rivers and streams and killing fish and other creatures. In trips back to her hometown of Springdale, she saw factories polluting the air, land, and water. In 1945, to her dismay, she saw the development of the atomic bomb, with its ability to destroy whole countries. In those concerns, she was not alone. Other naturalists and scientists had come to the conclusion that the natural world was threatened as never before. But those people were a minority. There was no environmental movement. If anything, there was a movement toward "better living through chemistry" and the increased use of chemicals in the environment. Several times, Rachel had proposed articles to prominent magazines about the threat to the environment from chemicals, but none showed any interest in the idea.

The Atomic Bomb

Scientists began working on the atomic bomb in the late 1930s. In June 1945, the first tests of the American bomb were conducted. Just two months later, the weapon would be used on a live target. On August 6, 1945, the United States dropped an atomic bomb on the city of Hiroshima, Japan. People at ground zero were killed instantly. Birds burst into flames in the air. More than 6,000 feet (1,829 m) from ground zero, paper caught fire in an instant. Experts believe that as many as 70,000 people might have died as a result of the initial blast. The long-term effects of radiation, which include cancer, could have pushed the death toll beyond 200,000.

POISON FROM THE SKY

By the late 1950s, scientists had developed more than 200 synthetic chemicals to kill pests such as insects, rats, mice, and weeds. Farmers, homeowners, and others spread millions of pounds of these toxic chemicals around the United States and the world. In the United States, the government and chemical manufacturers heavily promoted the use of pesticides. One widely publicized program of DDT spraying was aimed at wiping out gypsy moths on New York's Long Island.

A group of Long Island residents feared the spraying was potentially harmful. They brought a lawsuit against the local government to stop it. As part of the lawsuit, experts were asked to determine what might be the long-term effect of exposure to DDT on wildlife.

During her many years of research, Rachel had seen scattered

"All of these birds died horribly, and in the same way. Their bills were gaping open, and their splayed claws were drawn up to their breasts in agony."

– OLGA OWENS HUCKINS

reports about the poisonous effects of DDT on all wildlife. Now she followed the Long Island trial closely. Around the same time, she received a copy of a letter her friend Olga Owens Huckins had sent to the *Boston Herald*. Huckins wrote that DDT spraying to kill mosquitoes had killed the birds in her bird sanctuary. Yet the mosquitoes were worse than ever. "All of these birds died horribly, and in the same way," Huckins wrote. "Their bills were gaping open, and their splayed claws were drawn up to their breasts in agony."

Rachel, a bird lover, was horrified and deeply moved by the letter. It was the last push she needed to do something about what she thought was a growing menace. She approached publisher Houghton Mifflin and offered to write a book on the dangers posed by the widespread use of chemical pesticides. After some discussion, the publisher agreed.

Once again, *The New Yorker* editor William Shawn planned a two-part serial for the magazine. He encouraged Rachel to work tirelessly to uncover the truth about what pesticides were doing to the country. He had a strong belief that her writing might result in real change. "We don't usually think of *The New*

Rachel was an avid bird watcher who always carried a pair of binoculars with her on expeditions to the shore or the mountains. It was the sudden death and decline of bird populations that alerted her to the threat posed by the continued use of DDT.

Yorker as changing the world," he told her, "but this is the one time it might."

Rachel began talking to scientists, naturalists, and others about the effects of pesticides on the environment. She reached out to many people, from government officials to scientists to ordinary citizens. Toward the end of the year, however, her momentum stalled. On December 1, 1958, Rachel's mother died. She was devastated. All at once,

> **"We don't usually think of *The New Yorker* as changing the world, but this time it might."**
>
> – WILLIAM SHAWN

she'd lost her mother, her best friend, and her greatest supporter. Several days later, Rachel wrote to a friend about her mother:

> *Her love of life and of all living things was her outstanding quality, of which everyone speaks. More than anyone else I know, she embodied ... 'reverence for life.' And while gentle and compassionate, she could fight fiercely against anything she believed wrong, as in our present Crusade [against pesticide use]! Knowing how she felt about that will help me to return to it soon, and to carry it through to completion.*

THE CRUSADE CONTINUES

After her mother's burial, Rachel returned to her work with renewed energy. She collected hundreds of bits of evidence of DDT poisoning leading to death among birds, and illnesses—including cancer—among humans. The writing was slow. Rachel had hoped to finish the book by the end of 1959. But as the year came to a close, she was not even close. Worse yet, when 1960 arrived, Rachel found herself sidelined by a series of ailments, including ulcers and pneumonia. Then she discovered cysts in her breast. After doctors removed the breast, Rachel asked if the cysts were cancerous. The surgeon assured her that they weren't. Again, no further treatment was recommended.

In November, Rachel felt a new lump in her side. The lump was cancerous, and the cancer had spread. Rachel would need chemotherapy and radiation treatments. Both are incredibly harsh. Chemotherapy uses chemicals to attack cancer cells. Radiation therapy uses radiation to shrink tumors and destroy cancer cells. Unfortunately, both treatments also kill healthy cells and have brutal side effects.

> **"I just had the feeling at that moment that life had burned down to a very tiny flame that might so easily flicker out."**
>
> – RACHEL CARSON

The treatments left Rachel tired, weak, and often sick to her stomach. At times, the treatments made Rachel so sick that she was confined to a wheelchair. At her lowest point, Rachel described how she felt in a letter to a friend. "I just had the feeling at that moment life had burned down to a very tiny flame that might so easily flicker out," she wrote.

Worse yet, Rachel had reason to believe her illness could have been caught—and treated—earlier. When she had the first tumor removed in September 1950, Rachel asked doctors if it was cancerous. They assured her that it wasn't. Now Rachel suspected that the doctors hadn't been honest with her. In those days, doctors discussed a female patient's case with her husband. They did not always speak directly to the patient about her health. Rachel didn't have a husband and therefore didn't get all of the information. "Even though I asked directly," she told a friend.

Despite her weakened condition, Rachel was determined to forge ahead on the book. She and her editors tried to come up with a title. Though they considered many, none seemed right. Finally, Marie Rodell, Rachel's agent, came up with the perfect title. It was inspired by the book's opening, which read: "What has already silenced the voices of spring in countless towns in America? This book is an attempt to explain."

Even though she was a private person, Rachel was willing to stand in the spotlight if it would help bring attention to threats to the environment.

The book, which would be called *Silent Spring*, described the contamination of lakes, rivers, and oceans, and the death of countless life forms. It also contained a chapter called "The Human Price." In it, Rachel wrote:

> *Where do pesticides fit into the picture of environmental disease? We have seen that they now contaminate soil, water, and food, that they have the power to make our streams fishless and our gardens and woodlands silent and birdless. Man, however much he may like to pretend the contrary, is part of nature. Can he escape a pollution that is now so thoroughly distributed throughout our world?*

Rachel's answer, of course, was a definite "no." In the book, she went on to list example after example of ways that industrial pollution and pesticide exposure increased the chance of various types of cancer developing in humans. She ended the book with a plea for alternate methods of pest control that wouldn't involve the spraying of poison. In the chapter titled "The Other Road," Rachel wrote:

> *The choice, after all, is ours to make. If, having endured much, we have at last asserted our "right to know," and if, knowing, we have concluded that we are being asked to take senseless and frightening risks, then we should no longer accept the counsel of those who tell us that we must fill our world with poisonous chemicals; we should look about and see what other course is open to us.*

THE ATTACKS BEGIN

The first installment of *Silent Spring* appeared in *The New Yorker* in June 1962. Soon after its publication, lawyers for several chemical companies phoned the magazine. They said lawsuits would follow if the magazine ran additional installments. "Everything in those articles has been checked and is true," the attorney for *The New Yorker* responded. "Go ahead and sue." The next two installments appeared in the magazine as planned.

Even before Rachel's book was published, interest in the pesticide issue had spread across the country. During an August 29, 1962, news conference, President John F. Kennedy was asked about the subject. "Mr. President, there appears to be a growing

John F. Kennedy was the first president to hold regular press conferences. On August 29, 1962, he spoke about the threat of pesticides and the impact of Silent Spring.

concern among scientists as to the possibility of dangerous long-range side effects from the widespread use of DDT and other pesticides," said a reporter. "Have you considered asking the Department of Agriculture or the Public Health Service to take a closer look at this?"

"**Since Miss Carson's book, ... they are examining the [DDT] matter.**"

– PRESIDENT JOHN F. KENNEDY

"Yes," President Kennedy responded, "and I know that they already are. I think particularly, of course, since Miss Carson's book, but they are examining the matter."

The attacks on Rachel increased dramatically after the televised news conference. The chemical companies hired a public

The Presidential Science Advisory Committee was formed to advise Kennedy on scientific matters. Rachel (far left) was the only woman at a 1963 PSAC meeting.

relations company to present their side of the story: DDT and other pesticides were safe and *Silent Spring* was a hysterical attack against scientific progress. After Houghton Mifflin released the book in September, the controversy reached a fever pitch.

Rachel was ridiculed as a sentimental woman and a "fanatic defender of nature." In fact, most of Rachel's critics focused on her gender more than anything else. The words of former Secretary of Agriculture Ezra Taft Benson reflected what many of Rachel's critics were thinking. "Why [is] a spinster with no children … so concerned about genetics?" he wrote. Another critic wrote to *The New Yorker,* "Isn't it just like a woman to be scared to death of a few little bugs!"

> **"Isn't it just like a woman to be scared to death of a few little bugs!"**
>
> – ANONYMOUS

Silent Spring was officially published on September 27, 1962. In addition to the criticism, there was a lot of praise for the book. An editorial in *The New York Times* claimed that Rachel had written a story "few will read without a chill, no matter how hot the weather." United States Supreme Court Justice William O. Douglas called the book "the most important chronicle of this century for the human race."

Rachel received hundreds of fan letters. A number of scientists praised her accuracy and courage in writing the book. She also had a fan in the White House. President Kennedy announced the formation of a Presidential Science Advisory Committee (PSAC) to review government pesticide programs. Rachel was invited to testify before the committee. ❖

On an April 3, 1963 episode of CBS Reports,
correspondent Eric Sevareid interviewed Rachel about
the threat of unregulated pesticide use.

CHAPTER NINE

An Enduring Legacy

I T TOOK JUST TWO WEEKS FOR *SILENT SPRING* TO jump onto *The New York Times* Best Seller list. By the end of September, it was in the top spot.

In April 1963, Rachel appeared on *CBS Reports* in support of the book. The hour-long television show focused on the pros and cons of the argument presented in *Silent Spring*. Rachel was interviewed in her wood-paneled study. Sitting calmly in an office chair, Rachel spoke unhurriedly and naturally. It was a far cry from the image of a hysterical, angry woman being portrayed by her critics.

CBS also gave airtime to some of those critics. Chief among them was a biochemist named Robert White-Stevens. In contrast to Rachel, he seemed almost out of control. "If man were to faithfully follow the teachings of Miss Carson," he ranted, "we would return to the Dark Ages, and the insects and diseases and vermin would once again inherit the earth." By all accounts, Rachel won the argument in front of the television audience. Thousands of people from all over the country wrote to the United States government demanding that something be done about dangerous pesticides. The day after the broadcast, Senator Abraham Ribicoff announced senate hearings on the pesticide debate. Two weeks later, Rachel accepted an invitation to appear before the Ribicoff committee.

> **"All mankind is in her debt."**
>
> – SENATOR ABRAHAM RIBICOFF

On May 15, 1963, President Kennedy's PSAC released its report on pesticides. The report largely backed up Rachel's claims. Pesticides were poisoning America and the world. With the release of the report, CBS did a follow-up to its earlier television show. On it, Rachel said she felt vindicated.

The show concluded, "Miss Rachel Carson had two immediate aims. One was to alert the public; the second, to build a fire under the government. She accomplished the first aim months ago. Tonight's report by the presidential panel is … evidence that she has also accomplished the second."

Rachel was helping to win the fight against harmful pesticides. Unfortunately, she was rapidly losing the battle to save her own life. Despite the harsh treatments she endured, Rachel's cancer had reached her bones. By December 1963, she was confined to a wheelchair. Her life was ebbing away. On April 14, 1964, Rachel lost her battle with the disease. Senator Ribicoff marked Rachel's passing with the words, "Today we mourn a great lady. All mankind is in her debt."

HER SPIRIT LIVES ON

Today Rachel's legacy lives on. As a result of the outcry started by the publication of *Silent Spring*, the government established the Environmental Protection Agency (EPA) in 1970. The EPA was charged with the task of repairing the damage that had already been done to the environment. They were also responsible for providing new guidelines by which Americans could help create a cleaner environment. As part of its mission to protect human health and safeguard the environment (which includes land, water, and air), the EPA regulates ozone-damaging substances, such as auto emissions. It also bans certain harmful chemicals such as DDT, which was banned in 1972.

Saving the Bald Eagle

Many readers of *Silent Spring* were particularly disturbed to learn that DDT was killing off the very symbol of America, the bald eagle. DDT, which was found in large concentrations in the birds' tissues, caused them to lay eggs with very thin shells. The eggs were often crushed when the mother sat on them. Even eggs that were not crushed often failed to hatch. The symbol of America was in danger of disappearing. It wasn't until 1995 that the bald eagle was upgraded from an "endangered species" to a "threatened species." If DDT had not been banned, the bald eagle would almost certainly have disappeared.

On June 9, 1980, Rachel was posthumously awarded the Presidential Medal of Freedom. This is the highest civilian award given in the United States. When President Jimmy Carter presented the medal to Roger, Rachel's son, he read the following citation:

Never silent herself in the face of destructive trends, Rachel Carson fed a spring of awareness across America and beyond. A biologist with a gentle, clear voice, she welcomed her audiences to her love of the sea, while with an equally clear determined voice she warned Americans of the dangers human beings themselves pose for their own environment. Always concerned, always eloquent, she created a tide of environmental consciousness that has not ebbed.

DDT Makes a Comeback

After the United States banned DDT in 1972, most of the world followed suit. However, in 2008, the World Health Organization decided to back limited use of DDT as a way to control malaria. Every year, about one million people die from malaria transmitted by mosquitoes. Most of the victims are children living in Africa. In the early 1960s, malaria was almost completely wiped out in several poor countries. After the use of DDT was banned, however, the disease made a major comeback. Unfortunately, other, less harmful pesticides have so far proven ineffective.

Earth Day was first established on April 22, 1970. Since then, people around the world gather every year on that day to celebrate the gains that have been made in protecting the environment—and to fight for further progress.

Even though she died more than 45 years ago, the spirit of Rachel Carson, animated by her great love of the natural world, lives on in the worldwide environmental movement. Former United States Vice President and Nobel Peace Prize-winner Al Gore hopes to carry the torch of environmental activism that Rachel lit so brightly.

Like Rachel, Gore translated scientific fact into terms that most people could understand.

Always concerned, always eloquent, she created a tide of environmental consciousness that has not ebbed.

— PRESIDENT JIMMY CARTER

Rachel wrote a best-selling book to broadcast her message of pesticide danger. Gore used an Oscar-winning documentary, *An Inconvenient Truth,* to warn the world about the dangers of global warming. Gore warmly attributes Rachel with inspiring the movement that he now shares. He wrote:

> Silent Spring *planted the seeds of a new activism that has grown into one of the great popular forces of all time. When Rachel Carson died, in the spring of 1964, it was becoming clear that her voice would never be silenced. She had awakened not only our nation but the world.*

Thanks to her great love of nature—and steadfast dedication to preserving the natural world—Rachel Carson is known as the founder of the modern environmentalism movement.

An Inconvenient Truth

In 2006, *An Inconvenient Truth* shook the world in much the same way that *Silent Spring* did more than 40 years earlier. The documentary about global warming opened on May 24, 2006, and was soon drawing record crowds. In the movie, Gore reviews the scientific opinion on climate change and discusses the dangers it poses. *An Inconvenient Truth* also presents a call to action to all nations to cut the amount of greenhouse gases emitted into the atmosphere. The movie has spawned a growing movement to reverse global warming. It also won an Oscar for Documentary Feature for director Davis Guggenheim. Largely because of the success of the film, Al Gore shared the Nobel Peace Prize for 2007 with the Intergovernmental Panel on Climate Change.

It is true that Rachel Carson's voice was never silenced. In fact, its echoes can be heard at every Earth Day celebration and every time an animal is taken off the endangered species list. By refusing to give up or back down, Rachel created a legacy of caring and activism that extends from generation to generation. ❖

TIME LINE

1907   Rachel Carson is born on May 27.

1913   Rachel enters elementary school.

1917   The United States enters World War I. Rachel's brother Robert joins the Army Air Service.

1918   Rachel's first article is published in the September issue of *St. Nicholas Magazine*. World War I ends on November 11.

1925   Rachel graduates from Parnassus High School.

1925-1929   Rachel attends the Pennsylvania College for Women.

1929-1932   Rachel is enrolled in the master's program at Johns Hopkins University. She is awarded a master's degree in zoology on June 14, 1932.

1935   Rachel's father dies suddenly on July 6. Later that year, Rachel takes the federal civil service exam in the hopes of landing a job with the government.

1936   Rachel begins work with the U.S. Bureau of Fisheries in the beginning of the year. She is offered an official position as a junior aquatic biologist in August.

1937 Rachel's sister Marian dies of pneumonia in January. Rachel and her mother are left to care for Marian's daughters, Virginia and Marjorie.

1941 *Under the Sea-Wind,* Rachel's first book, is published. The United States enters World War II on December 8.

1945 World War II ends.

1946-1947 Rachel travels to Virginia to study waterfowl for her next book. She also travels to wildlife refuges in Utah, Montana, and along the Columbia River for the *Conservation in Actions* series she is writing for the U.S. Fish and Wildlife Service.

1950 Rachel finishes writing *The Sea Around Us,* her second book, in July. In September, she is hospitalized to remove a breast tumor. Rachel is awarded the Westinghouse Prize for excellence in science writing in December.

1951 A condensed version of *The Sea Around Us* is published in *The New Yorker* magazine. The story runs in three parts starting on June 2.

1952 *The Sea Around Us* wins the National Book Award in January. On April 7, Rachel is awarded the John Burroughs Medal for excellence in nature writing. Rachel resigns from the U.S. Fish and Wildlife Service effective June 3.

1955 *The Edge of the Sea,* Rachel's third book, is published. The book becomes a best seller.

1956 Rachel's niece Marjorie dies, and Rachel adopts Marjorie's son Roger Christie.

1958 Rachel's mother dies at age 89.

1960 Rachel is diagnosed with cancer and begins radiation treatments.

1962 Rachel's fourth book, *Silent Spring,* is published. The best-selling book raises the alarm about the dangers of chemical pesticides.

1963 Rachel appears on *CBS Reports* on April 3 to talk about the issues raised in *Silent Spring.* On June 3, she testifies before a Senate committee investigating the use of chemical pesticides.

1964 Rachel dies of cancer on April 14 at age 57.

1970 The U.S. government forms the Environmental Protection Agency (EPA) as a result of the public outcry inspired by *Silent Spring.*

1980 Rachel is awarded the Presidential Medal of Freedom on June 9. Her son Roger accepts the award on Rachel's behalf.

2007 Al Gore shares the Nobel Peace Prize for his efforts to educate people about climate change.

A CONVERSATION WITH

Carl Pope &
Albert Meyerhoff

Carl Pope (far left) is executive director of the Sierra Club. Albert H. Meyerhoff is a leading environmental lawyer. Both were inspired by Rachel Carson—together, they tell us how.

Q. How do you think Rachel Carson changed the world?

A. Carson's work provided the spark for the modern environmental movement. She demonstrated that one person can make a significant difference against a major polluting industry. That's incredibly inspiring.

Q. If Rachel were alive today, how do you think she'd view our response to our current environmental crisis?

A. We believe she would be saddened by the continued harm we do to the environment—the effects of global warming, the fight against clean energy, polluters dumping in our water, and more. Yet we also believe she would be pleased by the amount of people choosing to stand up for what they believe in: clean air, clean water, and communities safe from toxic chemicals. The environmental movement has become a major force around the globe today. That would probably inspire her as much as she has inspired us.

Q. What do you think the environmental movement would be like today if Rachel Carson had never written *Silent Spring*?

A. Congressional attention resulting from her book brought about a phaseout of DDT and later enactment of the first serious legislation to regulate agricultural chemicals. But *Silent Spring* did far more than just that. It created a change in consciousness that remains vital today. Because her book started such a movement, companies know they are held to certain standards. Environmental regulations as they are today would not be nearly as stringent had Carson never taken such steps to protect Americans from harmful chemicals.

Q. When young people read about Rachel's life, what lessons should they take away from their reading?

A. Despite the successes since Carson's battle, many major challenges remain. Since *Silent Spring,* pesticide use has increased at least tenfold. We add more than six billion pounds of these most toxic of chemicals to our world each year—nearly half just to kill weeds. If these chemicals were put in 10-pound bags and laid end to end, the line of bags would reach the moon.

Beyond pesticides, there are more than 80,000 chemicals now on the market. Virtually none have been tested for long-term human health effects. One recent study identified 216 different chemicals used in consumer products that cause cancer in animals.

Everyone's help is needed to protect the environment. Young people should know that everyone can make a difference, no matter what their age. They should also know that determination is essential.

Q. If you were to pick one outstanding virtue displayed by Rachel Carson, what would it be?

A. Carson's strength of character is most outstanding. Her unwavering determination in the face of such an opponent, in the face of so many attacks on her character, in the face of such a long road to regulation—it serves as a wonderful inspiration today.

Q. Rachel Carson's legacy is criticized by some today because the banning of DDT in Africa has led to an explosion of mosquitoes and a rise in malaria. Do you think this is a fair criticism? Why or why not?

A. Carson called for the careful use of DDT in fighting malaria—not a ban. Many non-toxic and less-toxic alternatives are available and affordable, such as cleaning mosquito breeding areas, use of treated nets, and early malaria detection and treatment programs. These methods can help treat malaria without exposing people to the dangers of DDT.

Q. If you could talk to Rachel Carson today, what would you tell her about the state of the environment?

A. We would tell her that she remains an environmental icon. We'd also tell her that, unfortunately, chemical companies are often up to the same tricks, and that other major corporations continue to push for polluting sources of energy, such as coal and oil. Finally, we'd tell her about the millions of people who fight for environmental protections, who fight against global warming, and who just genuinely care about each other and the planet.

GLOSSARY

abyss: an immeasurably deep gulf or depth in the floor of the sea

accolades: expressions of approval; praise

bathysphere: a steel diving sphere built by William Beebe and Otis Barton for deep-sea observation

bequest: a gift left by someone in his or her will

blight: a disease or an injury of a plant resulting in withering or stopping growth

botanist: a scientist who studies plant life

cytology: the branch of biology dealing with the structure and function of cells

DDT: a colorless and odorless chemical used as a pesticide that can accumulate in plants and animals

depression: a time of economic hardship that includes widespread unemployment

ecology: the branch of science that deals with the relationship between organisms and their environment

eloquent: vividly or movingly expressive

enthralled: held spellbound

eradication: state of being completely wiped out

exquisitely: pleasingly attractive or perfectly fit

fanatic: marked by excessive enthusiasm

ferocious: exhibiting extreme fierceness

grotesque: absurd or extremely ugly

habitat: environment in which a plant or an animal naturally lives

lean-to: a rough shed or shelter, often with a sloping roof

lilt: to sing or speak in a rhythm

malaria: a deadly human disease caused by a parasite and transmitted by mosquitoes

microbe: a microorganism undetected by the eye, usually a bacterium or virus

naturalist: one who studies natural history

oceanographer: a scientist who studies the oceans and their composition

philanthropic: characterized by goodwill or gift-giving

serialize: to break down a work into parts that follow one another

shoals: sandbanks that produce shallow water

stereotype: something conforming to a fixed or expected pattern

tentative: not fully completed or worked out, as in a plan

tide pools: shallow water left after the tide has gone out

zoology: branch of biology concerned with the study of animals

FOR MORE INFORMATION

BOOKS AND OTHER RESOURCES

Carson, Rachel. *The Edge of the Sea.* Boston: Houghton Mifflin Company, 1955.

Carson, Rachel. *The Sea Around Us.* New York: Oxford University Press, 1951.

Carson, Rachel. *Silent Spring.* Boston: Houghton Mifflin Company, 1962.

Carson, Rachel. *Under the Sea-Wind.* New York: Oxford University Press, 1941.

Lear, Linda. *Rachel Carson: Witness for Nature.* New York: Henry Holt & Company, 1997.

Bill Moyer's *Journal* on PBS did a retrospective on the life and legacy of Rachel Carson on September 21, 2007.

WEB SITES

The Life and Legacy of Rachel Carson
www.rachelcarson.org
This site has a wealth of information about Rachel, as well as information about the environmental movement.

The Rachel Carson Homestead
www.rachelcarsonhomestead.org
Rachel's childhood home is now a museum. This web site includes information about her childhood and other facts about her life.

The U.S. Fish and Wildlife Service
www.fws.gov/rachelcarson
The U.S. Fish and Wildlife Service has a web site devoted to Rachel Carson and her legacy.

SELECT BIBLIOGRAPHY
AND SOURCE NOTES

Carson, Rachel. *The Edge of the Sea.* Boston: Houghton Mifflin Co., 1955.

Carson, Rachel. *The Sea Around Us.* N.Y.: Oxford University Press, 1951.

Carson, Rachel. *The Sense of Wonder.* N.Y.: Harper & Row, 1955.

Carson, Rachel. *Silent Spring.* Boston: Houghton Mifflin Co., 1962.

Carson, Rachel. *Under the Sea-Wind.* N.Y.: Oxford University Press, 1941.

Lear, Linda. *Rachel Carson: Witness for Nature.* N.Y.: Henry Holt and Company, 1997.

Levine, Ellen. *Rachel Carson: A 2oth Century Life.* N.Y.: Penguin, 2007.

Wadsworth, Ginger. *Rachel Carson.* Minneapolis: Lerner Publications, 1992.

PAGE 2

The Sense of Wonder by Rachel Carson. Copyright © 1956 by Rachel L. Carson. Reprinted by permission of Frances Collin, Trustee, p. 67

CHAPTER ONE

Page 8, line 7: *Silent Spring* by Rachel Carson. Copyright © 1962 by Rachel L. Carson. Reprinted by permission of Frances Collin, Trustee, pp. 1–2

Page 10, line 4: *The New York Times,* July 22, 1962

Page 10, line 14: Lear, Linda. *Rachel Carson: Witness for Nature,* N.Y.: Henry Holt, 1997, p. 4

Page 11, line 1: Ibid.

Page 12, line 5: Matthiessen, Peter, ed. *Courage for the Earth.* Boston:

Houghton Mifflin Co., 2007, p. 63

Page 13, line 7: *Time,* June 14, 1999

Page 13, line 16: Ibid.

CHAPTER TWO

Page 17, line 6: Handwritten note of Maria Carson's, Rachel Carson Papers, Yale Collection of American Literature

Page 18, line 16: Carson, Rachel, "The Real World Around Us," speech, Theta Sigma Phi, April 21, 1954

Page 18, line 26: Lear, p.17

Page 20, line 7: Ibid., p. 9

Page 21, line 18: *St. Nicholas Magazine,* Sept. 1918

Page 22, line 13: Levine, Ellen. *Rachel Carson: a 20th Century Life,* N.Y.: Penguin Group, 2007, p. 22

CHAPTER THREE

Page 26, caption: Levine, p. 40

Page 29, line 6: Tennyson, Alfred Lord, "Locksley Hall," N.Y.: Penguin Books, 2007, p. 63

Page 29, line 9: Rachel Carson Papers

CHAPTER FOUR

Page 35, line 7: Lear, p. 60

Page 35, line 9: Ibid.

Page 36, line 14: *The Edge of the Sea* by Rachel Carson. Copyright © 1955 by Rachel L. Carson. Reprinted by permission of Frances Collin, Trustee, pp. 11–12

Page 38, line 9: Letter to Mary Frye, Rachel Carson History Project

Page 39, line 6: Ibid.

Page 41, line 12: Levine, pp. 60–61

CHAPTER FIVE

Page 46, line 16: Lear, p. 79

Page 47, line 2: Levine, p. 68

Page 47, line 3: Ibid.
Page 49, line 7: Sterling, Philip. *Sea and Earth: The Life of Rachel Carson*, N.Y.: Thomas Y. Crowell, 1972, pp. 88–93
Page 50, line 23: Edward Weeks to Rachel Carson, July 8, 1937, Rachel Carson Papers
Page 51, line 5: *Lost Woods: The Discovered Writing of Rachel Carson.* Copyright © 1998 by Roger Allen Christie. Reprinted by permission of Frances Collin, Trustee, p. 4
Page 53, line 12: Levine, p. 77

Chapter Six
Page 55, line 9: Lear, p. 90
Page 56, line 14: Ibid., p. 104
Page 56, line 20: *Under the Sea-Wind* by Rachel Carson. Copyright © 1941 by Rachel L. Carson. Reprinted by permission of Frances Collin, Trustee, p. 9
Page 58, line 11: Rachel Carson Papers
Page 62, line 6: Ibid.

Chapter Seven
Page 68, line 3: *The Sea Around Us* by Rachel Carson. Copyright © 1950 by Rachel L. Carson. Reprinted by permission of Frances Collin, Trustee, p. 13
Page 69, line 11: *The New York Times,* April 27, 1952, p. 1
Page 70, line 2: Rachel Carson Papers
Page 71, line 14: Carson, Rachel. National Book Award speech, Jan. 29, 1952, Rachel Carson Papers
Page 72, lines 2 & 6: Carson, Rachel. "Design for Nature Writing" speech, April 7, 1952
Page 75, line 11: Rachel Carson Papers
Page 77, line 5: *The Edge of the Sea* by Rachel Carson. Copyright © 1955 by Rachel L. Carson. Reprinted by permission of Frances Collin, Trustee, p. 11

Chapter Eight
Page 81, line 25: Huckins, Olga. *Boston Herald*, January 29, 1958 as quoted in Wadsworth, Ginger, *Rachel Carson: Voice for the Earth*, Minneapolis: Lerner Publications Co., 1992, p. 85
Page 82, line 11: Freeman, Martha, ed. *Always Rachel: The Letters of Rachel Carson and Dorothy Freeman,* Boston: Beacon Press, 1955, p. 125
Page 83, line 14: Rachel Carson Papers
Page 84, line 22: Freeman, p. 132
Page 85, line 5: Lear, p. 368
Page 85, line 10: *Silent Spring* by Rachel Carson. Copyright © 1962 by Rachel L. Carson. Reprinted by permission of Frances Collin, Trustee, p.1
Page 86, line 5: Ibid., p. 88
Page 86, line 20: Ibid., pp. 277–278
Page 87, line 5: Levine, p. 170
Page 87, line 12: JFK Library archives
Page 89, line 8: Lear, p. 407
Page 89, line 12: Levine, p. 167
Page 89, line 14: Lear, 419
Page 89, line 19: Ibid.
Page 89, line 21: Ibid.

Chapter Nine
Page 91, line 13: *CBS Reports*, April 3, 1963 transcript as quoted in Lear, p. 449
Page 92, line 16: *CBS Reports*, May 15, 1963
Page 92, line 27: Lear, p. 485
Page 94, line 5: Web site for the Presidential Medal of Freedom http://www.mcdaloffreedom.com
Page 96, line 6: Matthiessen, p. 67

INDEX

ABOUT THE AUTHOR

Charles Piddock is a former editor in chief of Weekly Reader Corporation, which publishes classroom magazines for schools from pre-K through high school. Charles has written and edited hundreds of articles for young people on world and national affairs, science, literature, and other topics. Before working at Weekly Reader, he worked in publishing in New York City, and, before that, served as a Peace Corps volunteer in India.

PICTURE CREDITS

Cover, p. 2, 96: Alfred Eisenstaedt/Time & Life Pictures/Getty Images; p. 6, 8, 70, 85: Associated Press; p. 12: Luke Frazza/AFP/Getty Images; p. 14, 17, 20: Carson family photo used by Permission of Rachel Carson Council, Inc.; p. 23, 24, 28, 51, 64, 76, 77, 88, 98, 100: used by Permission of Rachel Carson Council, Inc.; p. 26, 31: Rachel Carson Collection, Archives, Chatham College, Pittsburgh, PA; p. 32: Mary Frye, used by Permission of Rachel Carson Council, Inc.; p. 35: The Marine Biological Lab Archives; p. 38: Special Collections and Archives, the Milton S. Eisenhower Library, Johns Hopkins University; p. 40: Johns Hopkins University; p. 42: Hank Walker, Archive Photos/Getty Images; p. 44, 60, 73, 75: U.S. Fish and Wildlife Service; p. 48: NOAA; p. 54: Edwin Gray, used by Permission of Rachel Carson Council, Inc.; p. 56: Frances Collin/Yale Collection of American Literature, Beinecke Rare Book and Manuscript Library; p. 58, 63, 82: Shirley A. Briggs, used by Permission of Rachel Carson Council, Inc.; p. 61: Robert Brigham, Brigham Collection, Northeast Fisheries Science Center; p. 67: Brooks Studio, used by Permission of Rachel Carson Council, Inc.; p. 78: Bob Hines, used by Permission of Rachel Carson Council, Inc.; p. 87: Arnold Sachs/Archive Photos/Getty Images; p. 90: CBS Photo Archive/Getty Images; p. 95: Denis Paquin/ Associated Press; p. 101 Sierra Club.